The Dance of the Snow Tractors

ILLUSTRATED BY SHANNON WILVERS

Siena's Stories

The Dance of the Snow Tractors

Siena's Stories 1

ISBN: 978-1-989579-19-0

© Siena 2021

MotherButterfly
Books

www.motherbutterfly.com

This book is dedicated to
all the amazing front line workers
during the era of COVID-19.

My name is Siena.

I live in Ottawa, the capital of Canada.

My parents named me after a very pretty city in Italy.

Winter in Ottawa can be great.

We play in the snow,

build snow forts,

and make snow people.

However, winter can be tough on our neighbours.

Some people shovel their driveways.

Some of our neighbours
hire a snow blowing service.

First, they clear the driveways.

Then, the city grader clears the road.
It leaves huge mounds of ice and snow in front of all the driveways.
These large mounds have to be removed by the smaller snowblower.

Mom brings us hot chocolate.
We count the marshmallows and watch
the show all bundled and warm.

What happens next is my favourite part.

It's what I call the...

Dance
of the
Snow
Tractors

The small tractors return.

They zoom in and out
of the driveways removing
the left over mounds of snow.

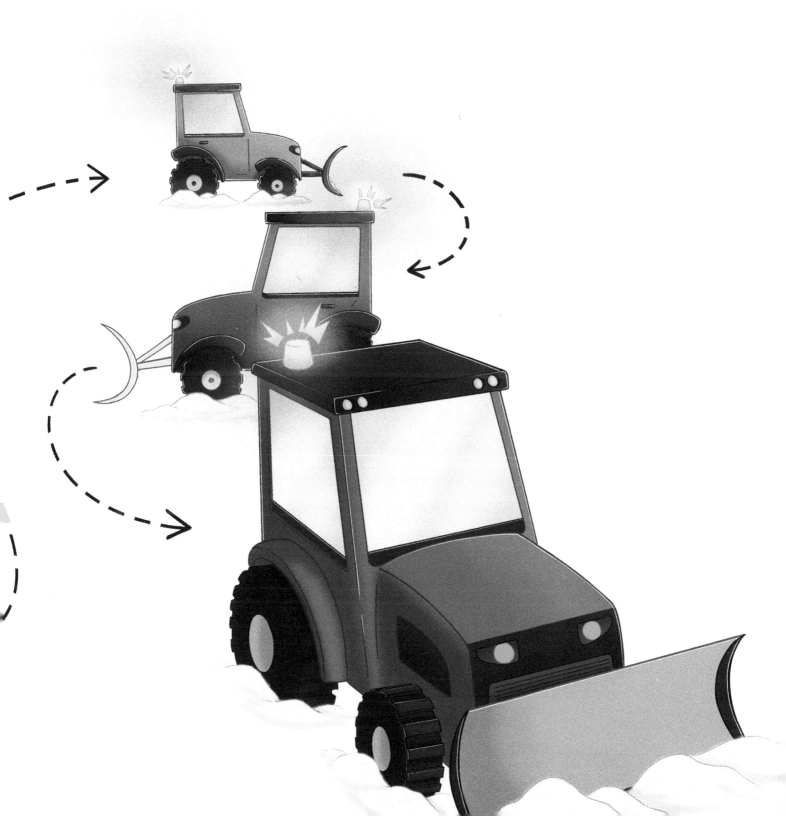

Another beautiful performance of the

Dance of the Snow Tractors.

About the Author

Siena is a real Canadian kid who likes hot chocolate and making up stories with her father. Both of whom choose to create these books somewhat anonymously.

About the Illustrator

Shannon Wilvers is a Canadian illustrator who loves drawing things on her computer. While she mostly draws and colours digitally, she also likes to experiment and play with different mediums such as watercolour.

In her spare time, she enjoys learning new things and watching cartoons. Her current favourites are "Avatar: The Last Airbender" and "Kipo and the Age of Wonderbeasts".

She is based in New Brunswick where she lives with her dog, Lucy.

If you enjoyed this book, please leave a review online at Goodreads & Amazon.

This is the best way for authors to share their stories with readers. We appreciate your help!

Thank you!

Enjoy FREE books!

GO TO:

motherbutterfly.com